DEATH WISH

I'm dying of cancer that alternate medicine **claims** it can cure,
why cure the cancer, when body **deterioration** I can't endure?

Suffering, **immobile**, requiring oxygen at every meal,
without life's pluses, does longevity's mere **existence** appeal?

Failing eyes & hearing, maxi-padded, intravenous fed, **better** dead
are fatal diseases a blessing or do some **relish** being spoon fed?

Are we so above the animals that we deny **designed** fate,
opting for extraordinary measures, **past** the 3 score &10 date?

Is the price of progress that we endure our **last** years in pain,
is it mortal sin to **exercise** freewill, before we go insane?

When we outlived friends & relatives that gave our lives **worth**,
is god a sadist to **exact** we suffer hell amid strangers on earth?

If criminals can **select** death, can't we take Kevorkian pills?
god forbid, what if someday medicare can't **afford** the bills?

Did primitive man in **compassion**, abandon elders to death,
has medical intervention gone **mad** in extending life's breath?

A depreciated parts bank, salmon returning to spawn,
cycle complete, moths fly to the light, life is withdrawn.

Energy's not lost nor gained but merely **transformed**,
atoms we were & to atoms revert, life **continues** reformed.

WHO-O-O PAYS the DUES?

J. LUNCHBUCKET

Order this book online at www.trafford.com
or email orders@trafford.com

Most Trafford titles are also available at major online book retailers.

Printed in the United States of America.

ISBN: 978-1-4269-4679-0 (sc)
ISBN: 978-1-4269-4680-6 (e)

Trafford rev. 11/15/2010

 www.trafford.com

North America & international
toll-free: 1 888 232 4444 (USA & Canada)
phone: 250 383 6864 ♦ fax: 812 355 4082

ACKNOWLEDGEMENTS

Thanks to hard won Workers' Compensation standards, my ears survived to glean some common sense from the Communists, Conservatives & Liberals at work that moulded me into the skeptic that I am.

Because of the old growth timber & leaders like Mark Mosher, George McKnight, Harry Kendall, Otto McDonald, David Burton, Aubrey Price & John Isaac that lead us to demand our fair share of the pie from McMillan Bloedel & other forest giants.

These Robin hoods were the knights of our round table & had they been Roman Catholics, they'd be candidates for sainthood. It was said that when the last Commie goes, so will our work standards.

Ask the survivors in our sunset industry, if this prophecy has come to pass.

PROLOGUE

The author has plagiarized the working man's blues. He was born & baptized RC but overcame this opiate dependency & worked on rails, grain elevators, offices, construction, fishing boats & logging camps.

This book satirically depicts taxpayers' burdens from the proletariat view.

Just like the opulent & degreed, wage slaves lacking university diplomas also have think tanks. Ours are in lunchrooms, bars & buses & boats used to go to work & home.

Workers don't just discuss sex in their daily 3 hour commutes, everything is on the table.

Workplaces are % representative & include the beaters, the beaten, child molesters, religious perverts, atheists, would be politicians, writer hopefuls or raconteurs that note the ranting of fools, prophets, lunatics & possibly unrecognized geniuses.

Within these pages could be the coded, unpolished gems that should be brought out of the dark & exposed to the light of day.

It's up to the reader to discern if the average Joe's simplistic approach to problems that governments appoint Royal Commissions for is laudable or laughable.

Do labour's grads of our rocky road's life possess the common sense that was brainwashed out of our Rhodes' scholars? Are we all equally adept at bull slinging & prone to greed & error like capitalists & intellectuals?

Where us & them differ is that workers don't patronize nor exude political correctness but let you know where to go, in as few words as possible.

This book is geared to the overtaxed lunchbuckets of the world & doesn't require a Mensa IQ, for comprehension on the first reading.

CONTENTS

LABOUR

POLITICS

COMMUNISM'S OBITUARY

Marxist theory "Each according to his **ability** & need,"
was to **feed** survivalists & allow high achievers to exceed.

With state banks, medicare, & education, capitalism **couldn't** compete,
before the world, godless socialism had to be brought **down** to defeat.

Overwhelming patriotism & altruism is mankind's **insatiable** greed,
free enterprise harnesses this Christian deadly sins to fill **its** need.

If Communism had accommodated this non simian **trait**,
we'd still have a socialist philosophy to which the poor **relate**.

Had USSR convinced the world to **shed** its dependency crutch,
would suicide bombers **heed** deities they couldn't see, hear or touch?

Capitalism's practical, **symbiotic,** moulded church & state,
bucks not greed nor gods, but **plays** the devil's advocate,
as army chaplains plug **oil** wars & the prince of peace desecrate.

If only the Kremlin hadn't cast faith, a forbidden fruit or **perversion**,
for priests coerced to work, communism was a **natural** aversion,
did RC collection plates proselytise Chile's Red state for **conversion**?

Whether the CIA **bought** the first non-Italian pope in 450 years is uncertain,
but this holy infallible weapon helped raise that **impenetrable** iron curtain.

For God & breathing space, we've **waged** war & millions died,
Red atheism failed because earthly **nor** heavenly rewards, could it provide,
in paradise dream we **choose** to confide so cold grave's reality is defied.

When Russia's Empire fell, of **real** freedom, Yugoslavia got a taste,
democracy's Christian crusaders, religious & ethnic cleansing embraced.
With no need for capitalism to **compete**, socialist gains were erased
& homelessness, the 21st century's free world's cities now faced.

In 2,009 capitalism's survival of the fittest, we had to **replace**,
corporate welfare was dispatched from public purse as a saving grace.
If governments **must** prop up failed corporations, why not buy them out
& **keep** private enterprises that work but socialism can we do without?

DEATH OF A COMMUNIST

Atheists have no **fear** of hell, yet some played it square,
dreams of **becoming** a millionaire they didn't share,
& died trying to create heaven on earth, paid **our** fare.
They never **darkened** any denomination's church door,
because the plight of the **poor,** church & state would ignore,
inequality & depression created communists & started war.

Reds were on a "do **not** hire" file, by corporations labelled hostile,
despite skill they were laid off, **short** of the 30 day period of trial.
As organizers, they faced **prison** or death by company hoods,
they missioneered cloistered in **bars** & secluded woods.
Sermons were **mass** meetings or pickets to lobby seats of power,
to raise **safety** & living standards & labour's dignity empower.

Through **wildcat** strikes & work to rule, things were done,
thus the 5 day work week by **illegal** means was won.

We all didn't share their **philosophy**, politics or faith choice
& even with **Red** baiting witch hunts, unions found voice,
but since the iron curtain has **fallen** on the Soviet empire,
bedbugs & bedrolls **return** to logging camps' bunkhouse fire.
After Communism fell, the **American** dream too, has died,
mental patients & drugged youth on today's city **sidewalks** reside.

We advised our Red friend to go to a cathedral for a miracle **healing,**
he said if he saw no prosthetic discards there, he **wasn't** kneeling.

If heavenly reward's path, is narrow & **straight** with no blacklist,
then our 29 day **wonders** will ascend the haven they missed.
If labour leaders are **locked** out & **good** works sin can't erase
& we're only saved by grace, must working class **hell** embrace,
can Christianity offer an **alternate** final resting place?

HOME GROWN REDS

The first **truism** Pravda*'s news did relay,
was "Red Empire crumbles in **decay**."
Teary eyes **glisten**, as Canadian Reds listen,
soon former **atheists** they will christen.
They discover that **their** god has died,
& that even party leaders had **lied**.

workers' funds hadn't kept their cause alive,
propaganda $ **enabled** foreign Reds to survive,
& helped unions achieve a **first** contract prize,
that previous attempts could **never** realize.

Had the CIA **bought** a Polish pope,
to put the iron curtain on a slippery slope?
If 11 **times** world sugar price, kept Cuba afloat,
did all these costs help sink the USSR **boat**?

Capitalism had **long** tried toppling it,
did corruption within, **eat** up Red credit,
was the failed experiment forced to **quit,**
is our corporate welfare & homeless a better fit?

*USSR newspaper

CATCH A RISING STAR – (Perry Como Tune)
(Survival In The Corporate Jungle)

Catch a rising star,
put him in your pocket,
never let him fade away,
lest you get a cut in pay.

For when your star's in motion,
you too may get a promotion.
But if you should **bungle**,
you'll be **alone** in the corporate jungle,
for alas, you have **no** voice
in making your new **boss'** draft choice.
You'll have to base your **reliance**,
in hope of forming **another** alliance,
& the predator instinct to **survive**,
you'll have to **revive**.

Catch a **new** rising star,
lock **him** in your pocket.
Tarnish peers, their **reputations** mar,
so that to the top, **you'll** rocket.
If you can't shine, this may be the **only** way,
to **prolong** your stay.

Catch a **rising** star,
get him in **your** pocket,
never let him fade away,
lest you lose your **steady** pay.

4

ENTRAPMENT

You may **think** your neighbour a friend "Tried & true",
until you work for him or he **borrows** money offa you.

After unreturned phone calls, on his door you rap & are **asked** in,
you try to **shame** him into paying, calling him a deadbeat before his kin.

Last Xmas as your employer he **gave** you a home-baked French pie,
this year to defend stained reputation, the ingrate **socks** you in the eye.

You dodge, push & lose your glasses as the **deadbeat** falls on his back,
with one hand on the stair rail, you're at his **throat** but don't attack.
It's his house so you let him up & he starts **throwing** punches again,
you're leaving the stairway dodging fists, the man is **frothing** insane.

As you reach the door, possessed he yells, "**You're** going to jail,"
you pick up your glasses, hasten to leave to **safeguard** your tail.

With no **prior** record, you stop at the cop shop, spout your tale of woe,
at this point it appears immaterial, that **you** didn't even strike a blow,
forcing a lie detector test on a **distraught** family, is a no go show.

The next day, you get a summons, charged with a **criminal** offense,
after reading three welchers' lies, you're a home **invader** without defense.

Not only are they reneging on debts, but they're **opportunist** scammers too,
this victim is backed up by a doctor's report & bodily **damage** will pursue.
If **God** is your witness & the blackguard has 2, the onus of proof is on **you**,
no righteous gene, no honor courses con veins, they smell $ & **sue** you.

Crown Counsel defends the shyster because **you're** charged with assault,
you all swear on the bible, can the **innocent** be judged at fault?

Courts are chambers of justice, **right** is not determined by might,
but just as in a democracy, the **majority** is deemed right.

"My **word** is my bond," not on everyone's conscience is engraved,
there's no debtors' prison nor mark of Cain to **expose** the depraved.

INSIDER BLUES – Johnny Cash
"Folsom Prison Blues."

Stuck in country club jail,
a chief executive **without** bail.
tennis & golf **gettin'** stale,
I **envy** jets' tail smokin' trail,
cause all I get's, **vir-tu-al** ma-le.

CHORUS :   I hear those planes **aflyin',**
                      tourist class & **first,**
                      I ain't **sellin'** nor abuyin',
                      it's freedom that I **thirst**.

I bet **workers** are adinin' on those flights,
boozin,' gamblin,' samplin' **forbidden** delights.
Did I really have it **comin'** to pay the legal fee,
or is shame of gettin' **caught** the **a-g-o-ny**?

Chorus:
My momma taught me **right** from wrong,
"Always be a **good** girl, don't sell it for a song."
Some say I dumped stock, **suckerin'** others to buy,
or a Judas **token** lamb on prime time, do they try?

Chorus:
CEOs **piddle** on peasants, media calls it rain,
good **lawyers** render crime a profitable gain.
Robbers netting less**, deserve** stiffer penal-ty,
it's style, the amount just tech-ni-**cal**-ity,
should white collar larceny **warrant** 3rd de-gree?

Chorus:
When they **spring** me from this cell,
is my soul **cleansed** & my demon no longer dwell?
Will I cry, "I've **seen** the light" or opportunity?
integrity's like lent, insider trades, pure **ecstasy,**
5 months on ice, isn't long but it **fr-eezes** me.

LIFE'S AMBITION – Sung To "Praise The Lord, I Saw The Light." Or "He's Got The Whole World In His Hands."

The working class can **kiss** my …, it came to **pass**,
I stepped up & made the **management** class at las'.
  The **prestige** of a company vehicle in front of the house,
  absences from home, at almost the **cost** of kids & spouse.
Trapped in the jaws of a vice, with security at a loss,
long hours, despised by workers & **bullied** by my boss.

  CHORUS: Cigarettes, nerve pills & bouts of **stress** leave,
    gave reprieve but **never** our choice did we grieve.
    Though we could discern **wrong** from right,
    we praised the lord for **our** right of might.

We're alphas & by nature, **genetically** endowed to lead,
the nature of our beast, **stoops** to any despicable deed.
  Plotting how our workers, we could **enslave**,
  contract out, drive them poorer to the grave.
Oh the staged dramas & **wicked**, tales we weaved,
practicing, so the arbitrator would be deceived.

Chorus:
From **lowly** foreman to super& manager, the pay increased,
& it was a strange quirk that **workload** had much decreased.
  Upon reaching the executive & board level, comes a **realizin'**,
  of full blown security & no fear of any **more** downsizin'.
For one hand washes the other, the board **executives** hires,
symbiotically, executives fulfil **directors'** wage desires.

Chorus:
CEOs, **seldom** in the line of fire, on big pensions retire,
corporate **hit** men for hire, downsizing **rewards** acquire.
  Even when we **quit**, the contract veritably fills our mitt
  &if we go in the **red**, for bad performance bonus is legit.
Survival of the fittest for employers of **size** no longer applies,
our press lies & corporate welfare averts enterprise demise.

Chorus:
Capitalism **won't** produce electric cars that don't use oil,
to profit, we **design** obsolescence, pollute & exploit toil.
　　Capital class & church-state dine off the **same** plate,
　　we're a symbiotic **soul** mate, with no equal to date.
Since **Red** empire fell, capitalism doesn't have to compete,
to quell revolt, we let homeless reside & **dine** on our street.

Chorus:
Politicians are stringed **puppets** in 21st century democracy
& moral majority hypocrisy bars atheists from **our** aristocracy.
　　We sell our souls & parasitically upon **labour** flesh, feast,
　　for profit, **crusades** are still aided by politician & priest.
We got the **whole** world in our hands at last,
middle class **death,** is by free trade forecast.

BAR FLY CHATTER

A recently divorced alkie confessed that he never knew what love was until he married & then it cost him ½ of what he had to get it back.
>>>>>>>>>>>>>>>>>>>>>>>>>>>>>>

In the 60's when Prince Rupert had 4 canneries on the Skeena River, population tripled in the height of the fishing season. When a new recruit walked into the bars, the girls off cannery row, **screamed** to welcome him. Every initiate in pants was an Elvis.
A naïve office lad that hadn't been broke in yet, made some righteous remark about the blatant promiscuity at a party. Miss cutie, one of the virtuous young lassies there, heard this & took **personal** affront saying, "**You** think I slept with everyone of these 20 guys here," well she pointed out at least 5 that she hadn't.
<<<<<<<<<<<<<<<<<<<<<<<<<<<<<<<<<<<<

I ran into one of my logging bunkhouse buddies. He was perturbed that I didn't recognize him. The sauce may have deadened some of my brain cells but 30 years ago, this was a tall lanky kid with a full head of hair. Today, in Archie Bunker vernacular, he's a bald headed good year blimp & the only thing that hadn't changed was his bubbling nice guy personality.
>>

The grandfather in the crew was telling us kids about some of the Haida massacres of other tribes & he was almost old enough to have been there. Our shell shocked WWII survivor who always butted in with his superior knowledge, added to the tale.
Grampa said "Did you see the sign outside the door?"
The WWII soldier says "No, what sign."
Grampa: park your bull outside.
>>>>>>>>>>>>>>>>>>>>>>>>>

One of the well healed sages at the adjoining table tells us that the only women that want to move in, have less $ than him. The successful ones just want a one nighter.
He rued not marrying young & settling for compatibility. Accumulating a modicum of success **first,** can turn us into self made recluses, seeking perfection & on finding it, face rejection or golddiggers.
<<<<<<<<<<<<<<<<<<<

We've been 2 months bushed in Rivers' Inlet & salivating for town.
Our buddy gets on the radio phone & pages one of his regulars in the Bucket of Blood hotel in Rupert & tells her he's flyin in for a week to see her.
His bar fly sweetie answers "I'll have my pants down," either not knowing or caring that every logging bunkhouse resident's only evening entertainment is the radio phone.
>>>

Another mark from work claimed he fathered 2 kids but raised 3. The youngest resembled the school teacher next door & boy was he smart compared to our peer that raised him. This sage in our forest that kept his brain from deteriorating by pickling it in spirits to maintain his 4th grade high level, was on another wife quest. This time he wasn't going to settle for anything less than a **professional** woman.

This simple Simon who shaves in a rose-coloured mirror is **still** single but did manage to rent a few pros in Vancouver.

>>>>>>>>>>>>>>>>>>>>>>>

One of the guys bragged that his girlfriend's parents bought them a dining room table.

When we dropped him off from the bar, we asked to see the table. He answered that it broke because it was designed for fulfilling only **culinary** fantasies.

<<<<<<<<<<<<<<<<<<<<<<<<<<<<<<<<<<<<<<<<<<

Nice guys are often marks & my Mark friend's mournful tale of 2 wives absconding with his assets didn't mention alimony, meaning he wasn't worth going after.

Mark may be a bit senile but still virile & hadn't totally given up on cupid. He announced his latest attempt which cost him $20.oo to join a computer-dating service.

His love match drove from Duncan to check him out. His rented one room cabin at Beaver Creek, obviously didn't con-pensate for his body beautiful & this madam of the chat lines never returned for another night of passion.

>>>>>>>>>>>>>>>>>>>>>>>>>>>>>>>>>>>>>>>

Ed, one of our top fallers, moved a bar fly in & tried to curb her boozing by not giving her any spending $.

One day, too windy to work, Ed invited us in for a drink.

It was 11 am & his princess left him a note that she was at the Somass bar. Ed couldn't figure out how she could barsit with an MT purse.

One of the crew let him down easy, saying "Ed, she's sitting on a fortune."

>>>

Steve, one of our crew put on the beef after fallers were forced off peace work to hourly rate.

He complained to us that his wife went through a change as well & he told her that he had more loving before they got married. She admitted that **she** did too.

>>>>>>>>>>>>>>>>>>>>>>>>>>>>>>>>>

DRUNKEN DUEL

A spirited home Valentine party, breaks out into a **drunken** duel,
lucking out with the gal of some other guy's choice, **sparks** the fuel.

Not wishing to **trash** the place, eagerly out to the street they depart,
disregarding blinding blizzard, pursuing **glory** in the pugilistic art.

Tumbling in snow-drifts, flinging drunken fists with few landing,
breathless from dodging cars, like mime **snow**-men they're standing.

Honour served, at length both decide to quit & call it a draw,
the aggressor offers a hand shake but as he turns, his flying **boot** we saw.

Marquis de Queensbury rules be damned, he **opts** for a kick in the crotch,
a dual purpose, to get him the girl & his opposition **debauch**.

Cold or the fear reflex, shrinks vulnerable testosterone to **miniature** size,
the intended victim grabs a foot, his foe falls back, not **targeting** the prize.

Covering **fallen** foe's eyes with his own shirt, he climbs his frame,
before administering the **last** rites, their buddies break up the game.

A **merciful** blow knocks him off, saving two lives much needless pain,
what an opportune time for friends' aid when one is temporarily **insane**.

Fair fights have **two** losers & night shift, masks one's black & blue shame,
the other explains to office secretaries that a **shiner** is part of the mating game.

EVOLUTION - proven

At birth all are baby bum **smooth**, even bald, later wrinkle & rust,
between teen & menopause is potency for **unadulterated** lust.

Puberty is bricks & bouquets – peach fuzz & **energizer** battery for boys,
girls get periods & breasts & poise, **opposite** sexes become play toys.

Men grow inches almost each time they meet the **loves** of their life,
shrunk & bowlegged at 60, we've lost 2 inches, **worn** out on the wife.

Menopaused women can lay back & **fake** it, freed of pregnancy fears,
male bones brittle & stiffen save **one**, battery weak, gone are best years.

No longer can the sheer power of **thought** raise it & double its size,
even with the real thing before it, its full potential **won't** materialize.
Standup routine falls, tailbone's broke & surgery won't bring relief,
when the **autonomic** primal response fails, it's just a hunk of beef.

The bulge between aging male legs is not of **romantic** intends,
one never knows when a pit stop is **required** so we pack attends.
Bones fracture, digits lose rigid, fate **worse** than death rears, we're steers,
with the discomfort of prostate checks, we **wonder** what's in it for queers,
can doctors legally charge **more** if a smile on their male patient appears?

Hourglass figures& chests that launched 10,000 erections, **droop** in defeat,
love juices dry & dread of non-performance **lessens** desire to cheat,
the tension has left the concrete, **resurrection** is a supernatural feat.

Even with inviagorating aids, a **rigid** digit is not a time guarantee,
we rue lost years of **self** deprivation when we were unattached & free.

Being at the food chain top, we have **no** predators to mercifully do us in.
bald, dark with old age spots, emaciated, **fat** is a face-lift for the skin,
when bathroom stops take **priority** over food & sex, is life a **win**?

We've played from the beginning to the bottom of the **last** inning,
hair thinning, head spinning, is merely **surviving** winning?

In an OAP recycle bin, we decompose **waiting** to rejoin deceased kin,
birthday suits stretched thin, we're skeletons **inviting** death's icy grin,
completing the circle of life, our **energizer** bunny has ceased within.

FORGIVENESS

A saintly atheist cared for her **dying** husband after 15 years away,
when even his mother & **siblings** thought him a mangy stray.

Left on dole to raise 5 kids alone, yet she **took** him back in,
do mortals exhibit divinity in pardoning **unforgivable** sin?

Do the scales demand balance or is vengeance outweighed by **love**,
will our maker be as **kind** & grant absolution in judgment above?

For **bloody** exploits & adultery, why wasn't king David stoned,
was his task on earth incomplete & penalty was **postponed**?

The author of "Amazing Grace" for many years was a **slave** trader,
was he saved by grace to become an ardent **abolitionist** years later?

Jamie **Braggart's** flock **forgave** him when he confessed he sinned,
did repentance he rescind, only to be caught **blown** in the wind?

Do we **revolt** & challenge the supremacy of a ruthless dictator,
or suffer & patiently await **after-life** justice from our creator?

Did survival of **fittest** or compassion get us to top of food chain,
must there be **more** givers than takers for the whole tribe to gain?

FUNERALS

Do our preachers always win, when they **pray** for a healing,
if patient recovers, is it all due to the **deity's** merciful dealing,
if not, does god take them unto her bosom, is death **appealing**?

I went to a **funeral** of one of the old gang, the other day,
& was flabbergasted by the grand **testimonials**, they did relay.
At last month's burial, the stiff also seemed **too** saintly for decay,
I wonder if my creditors will lie about **me** in so grandiose a way.
Such high praise, as if they were all born free of **original** sin,
envious, I almost wished **I** was the worm food in that **coffin**.
But even if the unholy corpse didn't **deserve** any applause,
his farewell was for a forgiving family or one **blind** to his flaws.

Humanely we put our animals down saving them agony & pain,
but in our final years, past lifestyle we're **unable** to maintain.
Clergy say "'tis a far better place we go, than this **mortal** plane,"
yet by any means **they** delay death, doubting after-life is a gain,
is medical intervention to prolong our stay **not** insane?

Evolutionists state that **genetically** apes are our peer,
but did the creator, a **dependency** faith gene engineer?
If the good lord answers all prayer, why **seek** doctor care,
have faith, **not** works nor arms we bare but by grace, we fare.
Is religion a crutch, robbing our **reason** & ability to think,
does it **soften** cold grave reality, is it our **choice** opiate drink?

HAIKUS

Evolution or creation,
man's plaguing vexation,
cremation or salvation?

Realize we are,
started from stuff of star,
man & god at par.

We think & are of worth,
imagination gave gods birth,
devils reside on earth.

Are gods sugar-pills,
grist for our mind mills,
atheists - steel wills?

Logic or deification,
dogma or determination,
ignorance or education?

Reality or crutch,
gods not to see nor touch,
tithing - too much?

Crutch or reality,
superstition or morality,
death a finality?

Pagan abomination,
man-made god or creation,
grave destination?

After-life idealized,
pagans proselytized,
gods downsized.

If war is distressing,
& killing requires confessing,
why papal blessing?

Civilization's run,
takes a backward step in WW I,
power is from barrel of gun.

15

Genes govern longevity,
after-life there may well be,
but death is certainty.

Go forth & multiply,
cannon fodder supply,
environment defy.

Life in paradise,
puppies never grow old,
dependence is sold.

Hawaii's gene base,
is a blend of many a race,
KKK has no space.

Lumber was our industry,
till we exported old growth tree,
today grass is an industry.

Keep off the grass,
don't eat cookies of hash,
sell the crop for cash.

Nature in the raw is sex,
celibacy unnatural & complex,
but population it checks.

In paradise we were all nude,
yet preachers label nudists lewd,
is cultured society a prude?

Friends made in foul weather,
prove as durable as tough leather,
wear well & light as a feather.

If conceived in sin,
to go forth & beget kin,
is chastity a no win?

LAST RITES

Is euthanasia **condoned** when we starve the terminally comatose,
but a **criminal** offence if these patients, we purposely overdose?

Is out of sight, out of mind the **modern** day morality,
if we disregard patient **suffering**, is society stuck on legality?

We won't **all** be granted a painless passing, in the dream state,
must we endure past lives' karma, **awaiting** death's date?

Must workers never by pain & disability **encumbered**,
prolong the agony of decreased quality, when days are numbered?

We have wills & testaments to bequeath to kin, our **lives'** net worth,
shouldn't choice to shed life's burden be a legal **right** of birth?

If condemned prisoners can **opt** for life sentence or quick death,
must we, pain interned, be **forced** to draw our last breath?

Doctor-assisted suicide is as humane as **penitentiary** execution,
shouldn't good Samaritan acts be **enshrined** in the constitution?

Can we not **opt** for the Kevorkian solution,
if it's not coerced & witnessed, won't god grant **absolution**?

If a healthy foetus has **no** right to conception,
of Solomon's **wisdom**, has our judicial system any perception?

Hitler's Germany **enforced** euthanasia & sterilization,
will **we** resort to wars or legislation to curb overpopulation?

LIFE TERM

It's been nigh **thirty** years of stability,
my independence I had **traded** away.
Saddled with duty & responsibility,
no time to stray, or confidence betray,
no chance to **sample** life's buffet.

When I see a **rubbie** right after his fix,
eyes glazed, **ecstasy** to the nth degree.
I wonder if my spouse got **her** kicks,
on the **challenge** in me that she did see?
Had she met a good man, where would **I** be,
could **that** unfortunate druggie be **me**?

Loss of freedom, chained to **one** wife,
by Hollywood standards, it's a **curse**.
My peers' consolation **cuts** like a knife,
"She stepped down, **you** would have fared worse."

MY WILL

Dearest family, to put it bluntly, I changed my will,
the black hole you stuck me in, my needs doesn't fulfill,
if I linger longer, I'll have to take my Kavorkian pill.

In this dumping ground, you abandoned me all alone,
to sit, contemplate my fate & for my frugal past atone,
just an old crone dying among strangers, largely unknown.

No beer spout here, this dry home suffers constant drought,
your lives are busy no doubt & you mostly counted me out,
to give all a goal so each pay the toll, I leave you without.

My will, not thine, since I'm the one that made the dough,
I've outlived many peers & have old timer's, this I know,
but your new stepmother & I hit an **enlightened** plateau.

We'll trade hereafter's middle man church tithes, for **now**,
too long we've sweated & slaved chained to the plow,
no more theory, nor do we pray or bow, **reality** we vow.

No more on Vallium to rot, better to be strung out on pot,
no hippy ever died from massive heart attack or blood clot,
we're pooling assets & **selling** the burial plot we bought.

We're buyin' a Harley & goin' on a North American tour,
then chartering a fishboat to rinse off that farm manure,
we'll procure these treats for sure, it's a boredom cure.

Then to slash cash cost, on a cruise we'll blow our stash,
it may well be our kick the bucket list, last bash,
like lemmings, our dash may end in a big sea splash.

Too long we've laboured, saved, been virtuous & devout,
we're virtual prisoner here, with no power or clout
& soon as we decipher the door code, we're **bustin'** out.

PRIMORDIAL URGE

Full blown rut dissipates modesty & inhibition, **overpowers** the brain,
the mating instinct **outweighs** self-preservation, driving males insane.

The male spider 1/5th his mate's size, **courts** the jaws of certain death,
is reincarnation achieved possibly at cost of **drawing** his last breath?

Is it noble sacrifice or for genetic immortality an **equitable** trade,
no regrets, by his flesh, **nature** designed how arachnid eggs are laid.

The animal kingdom risks demise & the **fittest** achieve insemination,
does agrarian excess allowing inferiors to **breed**, weaken creation?

Evolution of vocal chords separated us from our hairy simian kin,
but with less than 2% DNA variation, is difference **membrane** thin,
do we **know** that we have soul, or does the primordial beast, beat within?

VANCOUVER WHORE – Sung To Randy Travis' "3 Wooden Crosses"

Parasites living off the **avails** of shame,
    the pimp **displays** his painted dame,
    professionals in the world's **oldest** game.

A shadow cast figure, **neon** lit face,
    She's **any** woman, of every race.

A hedonist out for **kicks** not through necessity,
    a **working** girl with no option, deserving pity?

CHORUS: Vancouver **whore**, slim & slender,
                  seemingly innocent, young & tender.

Someone's daughter, sister or **even** wife,
    did you knowingly **choose** such a life?

Granville Street, the **height** of your profession,
    & the start of your **ultimate** regression.

You endure the lows to **soar** on high,
    you're 21st century's **vampire** & death defy.

When the **next** trick may be your last,
    your life's a blast, pace **fast** cast.

Chorus:
You **degenerate** from a great looker,
    to a Hastings Street **needled** hooker.

another pro off skid row, fallen from grace,
    drugs & **sadness**, etched in your face.

In the end when you **meet** your maker,
    will your sentence be, **hell's** half acre?

Chorus:
When peers succeeded with **half** your ability,
    will your excuse be bad **luck** & abuse by family,
    denying a life out of tune was cause of misery?

If to judge, is **not** for mortal man to do,
    but for the **one** that created me & you,
    will **rich** & famous addicts too, get their due?

AUTHORS

To market a lie of **biblical** proportion,
dampen dissection, inspection & correction,
claim authors' **divine** inspiration & connection.
Burn heretics claiming bible is **man's** distortion,
scare hell into believers into **tithing** extortion.

It's **not** a novel idea, it's all been done before,
seed **doubt** & innuendo, offer lost souls to restore,
church-state **symbiosis** ensures you an open door.

The more critics, the more **media** exposure,
only **death** threats signal you're past kosher,
notoriety translates into **sales** with no closure.

Label your **serial** old & new testament books,
sprinkle chapters & verses with **clues** & hooks,
shroud controversy in **mystery** for faith kooks.

Impose health rules & diets they **must** follow,
even if the dogma is now **obsolete** & hollow,
promises of **everlasting** life, they'll swallow.

If faiths' **dependence** opiate offers to save,
but the alternative is the reality of a **cold** grave,
will believers drop crutches or **dare** misbehave?

Over time establish a monopoly on **your** truth,
claim infallibility, direct ideology at youth,
claim absolution's only at **your** confession booth.

If science challenges religion, **revivals** engineer,
threaten that Armageddon's **rapture** looms near,
give sinners a pardon by **grace,** to allay their fear.

Church state **supports** presidents that god talks to,
if politicians step out of atheist **closets,** they're through,
just as in McCarthy **era,** Red & godless is still taboo.

The world spins & almost **nothing** forever remains,
shine new light of revelation & **baffle** brains,
to counter heresy, inquisitors go to **great** pains.

CRYSTAL CATHEDRAL

Crystal cathedrals, immortality pyramids of **righteous** men,
twisted priorities, **ego** monuments, spiritual exploitation, amen?

Bible forbids graven images, **our** mansions are in the sky,
do **messiahs** disregard gods' good books & focus on the 'I'?

Faith peddlers for themselves & **their** kin, church pulpits secure
& exploit parishioners' vanity as **name** plaques they procure.

Like feudal chiefs, it's **nepotism's** privilege for the few,
hard work & tithing, only **after**-life rewards accrue me & you.

"Train up a child in the way it **should** go & they won't depart,"
families that pray together, **profit** in the family business they start.

Charity begins at home, their pets **air**-conditioned doghouses get,
while the flock atone for **their** sins, bathed in honest worker sweat.

If ambition driven corporate executives function **best** on commission,
should pastors be denied a % for **increasing** the flock of the mission?

To maintain the **style** of living they're accustomed to, they persevere,
are we lead by shepherds, whose soul vocation is a **lucrative** career?

A dependence gene may render **televangelists'** messages divine,
but off **taxpayers'** flesh all holy shrine dine, atheists can't decline.

DIVINE EVOLUTION

To survive each day, did hunter-gatherers have **time** to pray,
or did **superstition** become career after agriculture's buffet?
Before society evolved a justice system, were **gods** needed,
would only an **all** seeing **vengeful** deity by most be heeded?

If **goddess** figures were the first of anthropologists' finds,
did patriarchs switch to a **male** figure to enslave our minds?
Ancient immortals were **territorial**, warlike, loving & prolific
& prayers for rain or **fertility** were directed to the deity specific.

Religions wavered from polytheism to worship of **one** unseen god,
were rulers **awed**, or was this control tool unadulterated fraud?
In monotheism was our dependence **opiate** styled & moulded,
did angels & saints **fill** the pagan void as other entities folded?

Did a plagiarized demi-god of **virgin** birth replace animal sacrifice,
did Christ, the lamb of god become humanity's **ransom** price?
Limbo, purgatory, hell & heaven, **life's** deeds have wrought,
by papal decree for fee, damned souls by **rich** kin were bought.

Among our simian kin, the leader is the **strongest** in the tribe,
did we **evolve** a faith gene to pray & consult intermediary scribe?
Was the bible's authenticity by **priests** invented & conspired,
so mortal man would never question words **divinely** inspired?

If **imagination** fueled ghosts, goblins, fairies & UFO,
did the devil become the **fall** guy for all of mankind's woe?
Did we buy into after-life to deal cold grave & **reason** a death blow,
are tithes insurance, can anyone know that we **reap** what we sow?

Infallible pope & **divine** right of kings, was to church-state revised,
has a superior **symbiosis** of Caesar & pulpit ever been devised?
Popes preserved their monopoly with **heretic** burnings & inquisition
& **chaplains** blessing crusades, became a fundamentalist tradition.

When fellowship is wanting, do revivals **lure** with dance, music & song,
does fear of rapture, **ante**-Christ & 2nd coming, terrify us to belong?
Did deity vanity demand "Thou shalt have no other gods before me,"
will fundamentalist majority **bar** agnostics & atheists from US democracy,
is Mao's echo "Religion is a **poison**," prophecy & 21st century reality?

MESSAGES FROM BEYOND

I'd like to get a message from my own dearly departed,
in hindsight would they have altered course & life recharted?
Any word would be welcome from black sheep, friend or foe,
a reply could determine how the rest of **my** life should go.

Nothing's ever been heard from anyone that's gone on before,
no word has come from beyond, did they enter heaven's door?
Biblical scroll & hell hole damnation, can we afford to ignore,
do tithes only employ clergy's store or points in hereafter score?

Should we reform & go out of our way to perform saintly deeds,
is it too late because **collectively**, we sow too many wild seeds?
Was missionary position a matter of preference or land acquisition,
is it right of might ambition to elicit god in just oil war expedition?

Is religion an **opiate** of masses & church-state, a tool of control,
should stewardship & planet preservation be our **primary** goal?
Can prayer & faith or **technology** deliver us from asteroids' toll,
are we really above animals or **vain** to claim that we have a soul?

Unions opt to create heaven on earth & don't **buy** pie in the sky,
celibacy advocates to forego earthly pleasures for the by & bye.
If preachers don't hasten departure nor medical intervention defy,
do they secret **insider** knowledge that to parishioners they deny?

Necromancy* was banned by R.C. papal infallibility decree,
but until the withered branch off family tree, **confirms** eternity,
will I buy into preachers' "meek will inherit the earth" philosophy,
in this reality, I treat others as I wish to be & please mainly **me**.

If beyond the grave we all could see, would any incur penalty,
would we agree to live righteously & gain after life's guarantee?

*Necromancy – conferring with the spirits of the dead.

MISSIONARY POSITION

How much testosterone is required to maintain the **missionary** position,
if gods can't be seen, heard nor felt, **why** go on a proselytizing mission?

Is blind belief needed to deify a demi god of virgin birth, **2,000** years ago,
was **prime** directive conversion or annex land, what does record show?

Colonialism's cross went on before, **slaughtering** pagans by the score,
will the prince of peace usher in Armageddon's rapture & **peace** restore?

Did popes adopt heathen holidays to **cement** religious coalition,
is purging **heresy** by inquisition & chaplains blessing crusades, tradition?

Do we save souls there may **not** be & erect monuments of immortality,
is secular humanism to be labeled for all time, the **enemy** of theology?

Is it a must that in god we trust**,** do we require **more** than laws & rules,
are we destined to forever be willing church-state servants & tools?

Does a faith gene or opiate **lock** us into religious **co-dependency**,
is it **hypocrisy** to promise paradise & deny grave's death reality?

NEW JERUSALEM – "Oh Come All Ye Faithful"

God's chosen & crusaders tried to seize the **promised** land,
will this site be Armageddon's rapture & humanity's **last** stand?
When the Lord looks **down** upon her holy city of Jerusalem,
are **pilgrims** or bombs at wailing wall, can we stop the mayhem?

Since the almighty won't **intercede** on earth as an arbitrator,
can **greed**, one of the 7deadly sins be our millennium motivator?
Cities have **embellished** legends of Loch Ness, yeti & UFO,
in exploiting 3 major holy places, can monetary **blessing** flow?

CHORUS: Oh come all ye faithful, buy **shares** in Jerusalem,
                    an **oasis** in a desert of atheism, is the holy land gem.
                    a walk on water test & hope for a **new** age ecstasy,
                    a port in a storm, mecca start on a **peace** prophecy.

If Jews, Christians & Moslems can **profit**, they'll war no more,
uncover new holy digs, as **playgirl** bunnies vie for temple whore.
As ethical as sales of **indulgences** or planned obsolescence,
market pilgrimage **atonement** for elders & holiday for adolescents.

Build it & not pillaging crusaders but paying tourists will come,
in a meditative trance, to guilt & tithing they will **succumb**.
Post faith **healings** & saints' relics, on the internet advertise,
exorcise demons, flog heaven's **time** shares, proselytize & baptize.

Chorus:
To keep the pews filled, patronize & **offer** dance, music or song,
media can showcase that diverse fundamentalists **can** get along.
God is not obsolete, the masses' opiate is **codependency** forever,
religion & capitalism is a winning team we must **never** sever.

Cease **psychiatric** analysis of stigmata messiahs in Rome,
promote **second** comers, afflicted by the Jerusalem syndrome.*
1st commandment states "Thou shalt have **no** other gods before me,"
but democracy decree gives all a **freedom** of worship opportunity.

Chorus:
Christ was crucified on the cross, man's **everlasting** life to buy,
Xmas & Easter fuel sales **demand,** that entrepreneurs happily supply.
Jerusalem is a **holy** cow to be **milked**, insure she never runs dry,
if spirit needs revival, can we **deify** another lamb to crucify?

*Jerusalem syndrome – psychiatric condition where patient believes he's Christ reincarnated in a 2nd coming.

PAGAN RITES (growing up RC)

A Sunday school teacher at **Easter** read:
"Christ came **back** to life from the dead."
"**That** can't be true," an innocent 5 year old said,"
can it be that **common** sense is in all inbred
& **washed** out by the fundamentalist diets we're fed
to **reject** cold grave reality & buy heaven's dream instead?

Catholic nun **teachers** made their young students' heads spin,
saying "Protestants may be **nice**, but to heaven they won't get in."

Eating meat on Friday, was for Roman Catholics a **sin**,
said a teen to his mother, "If that be my **worst**, paradise I'll win."

Does society **bend** minds like saplings to mould the tree
& church-state chaplains **inject** opiate to spur crusaders to victory?

Did "Thou shalt have **NO** other gods before me," ensure monopoly,
is religion faith **gene**, poison or control tool of church-state theocracy?

Are the odds in favour of winning in a casino or lottery
compared to threat of eternal hell or heaven's guarantee?

How much testosterone is required to **maintain** missionary position,
if gods can't be seen or heard, **why** go on a proselytizing mission?

Can we label other beliefs "**pagan** mythology" & only ours revere,
if televeangelism wasn't a **lucrative** career, would anyone volunteer?

Is it **hypocrisy**, that only to prophets & kings god will talk,
does our dependency blur reason & we **forget** we can walk?

Democracy's freedom of worship breaks the 1st commandment "Thou shalt have no other gods before me." Let he who is without sin, stone this blasphemer.

THE RHYME OF THE MODERN MARINER -
Plagiarized Samuel Coleridge Taylor's "Rhyme Of The Ancient Mariner," Killing Of An Albatross.

In a smoke-**stained** far below par, light depraved bar,
at this bizarre bazaar, addicted I puffed on my **last** cigar.
Amid the **shadows** of lost souls amid the human debris,
abruptly, a washed-up sea dog staggered in & **collared** me.
In vain, he tried to link & get us **practised** alkies to think
he sailed that slimy, salty sink **without** a drop to drink.

He held us captive with tongue & **withered** hand,
uttering words, we cast-offs **couldn't** understand.
Of the International **World** Counsel of Churches'
relentless, mostly fruitless land & sea searches
for long hidden **alien** writings & artefacts,
that had **curbed** men's blood-thirsty, barbaric acts.
Of perceived **angelic** passed-on information,
that **inspired** prophets from each & every nation,
to **institute** a deity to stifle our inborn greed,
& seed some compassion into that **primeval** breed.

He spoke of those **beings**, 3000 years later returning,
finding materialism, was still society's **constant** yearning.
Church & state occupying the same **incestuous** bed,
poisonous as serpent Satan, **perverting** humanity instead.
For in the **almighty's** name, there's ethnic killing,
exploiting faith & patriotism, nations are still willing,
for oil, presidents get **divine** counsel & justify killing.

"These starry messengers **played** with our mind,
the **message** they relayed was not kind.
If man won't turn from **religious** hypocrisy,
in the next millennium they'd **again** curb our lunacy."

"With **ungodly** strength, those puny aliens we did kill,
our **dedicated** Luddite vocations we did fulfil.
In the name of the one that died on Calvary's **cross**,
we salvaged our careers & **sunk** the UFO 'Albatross.'"

"For what **worth** are faith peddlers without a God,
are we **nude** emperors & an unseen entity laud?
Should tithing be exposed as **unadulterated** fraud
& preachers be pressed into **manual** labour to plough sod?
Since that fateful day, my thirst's not **quenched** by water,
the **devil's** brew has become my **daily** fodder."

The recount of his bloody deed, cast a spell & **mesmerized,**
spellbound, patrons of the strip arts sat veritably paralysed.
Obsessed, he bent our ear, in fear we were **bound** to hear,
he glowed in beer, proselytised we **recognized** a kindred peer.
But as the wretched **wild**-eyed, old bloke spoke,
all us derelicts squatting there, spotted his **soiled** yoke,
for a tattered **collar** 'round his neck, the ole alkie wore,
forsooth, in truth, he **had** been a cleric, that son of a ….

Still spewing terrifying consequences of **foreboding** swill,
with orator skill, the old mariner **dominated** our will.
He bade us swear an oath to eradicate **spiritual** idio-sin-cracy,
save man **not** souls & cease erecting monuments to immortality.
Stop dealing spirtuality dependency, establish a **global** democracy,
curb our propagation & ensure **all** species' sustainability.

"A **sterile**, non-polluting united world , those ETs should see
for if Sodom & Gomorrahs there **still** should be,
rapture would spare other creatures from **sacrificial** penalty,
only **humanity** would be purged in a cleansing fire of ecstasy."

If you **doubt** & balk at swallowing this revelations' tale,
quaff & buy me yet another bitter ale & **raise** history's veil.
Contemplate the innovation of Guttenberg's **printing** press,
no longer a biblical **monopoly**, did infallible popes possess.
Truth, no longer could they suppress or get all to confess,
competition, holy mother church now had to address.

If no gods are seen, heard or touched, since **time** began,
what need there be, of a missionarying **clerical** clan?
Just suppose that if all immortals were **proven** dead,
where would all those religious **perverts** head?
How would nations ever be able to wage a **just** oil war,
without chaplains **blessing** troops to open heaven's door?
What would they do with all that **wasted** praying time,
spend it here with us & get out of **white** collar crime?

To colonize new worlds with the **fittest** few,
would theologians or **pioneers** be the chosen crew?
Reality's a cold grave & **heaven's** dream, sublime,
menial work's honest, **low** caste, not romanticised like crime.
Sheltered & fed here, we **savour** the arts, it passes the time,
but will your belly fill on flowery swill, **sermons** & rhyme,
are priests & poets drones & **worth** a goddamned dime?

XMAS

CHORUS: Busy sidewalks, shoppers we be, it's **great** for the economy,
every girl & boy, holidays **enjoy** with presents under their tree.
Indoors we reside when the weather **outside** is so frightful,
we dream & **perspire** by the hearth fire, it's oh so delightful.

Children laughing, smile every aisle, it's **Xmas** time in our city,
3rd world is not so pretty, thirst & **hunger** is a global pity.
To proselytize without a fight, Christians adopt a **pagan** rite,
to celebrate Christ's birth on earth, Dec 25 becomes **holy** night.
Priest & politician reconcile & **patronize** each other's position,
holiday transition evolves into a paid union-**capitalist** tradition.

Chorus:

Amen, good will to men, peaceably on earth, this season **we** abide,
as loners & crackheads rally in **needle** alley & contemplate suicide.
Silver bells, snow's glistening spells soon, our kids' **favoured** day,
pipers piping, dopers **shooting**, skids celebrates in their own way.
As winter's chills, victims kills outside a Sally-Ann flop **chalet**,
drunk & bleary toast their host, surviving yet another **holy** day.

Chorus:

The die is **caste**, we're walking in a winter wonderland of contrast,
rich-poor gap we endure, it **widens** fast, can the middle class last?
Chills of closing mills, fills New year with ghostly bills of Xmas past,
sting they bring, are we overstuffed Buddhas in **dire** need of fast?
Is it luck or **karma**'s fee, that separates homeless from me & thee,
jobless depression leaves impression, we **all** can be human debris

Chorus:

USSR communism was realism, by **rations** the hungry got bread,
Red seduction was to **own** the means of production so all had a bed.
Jingle bell, time will **tell**, socialism for the lower class is long dead,
trickle down theory we're fed but corporations get welfare instead.
Is free trade best to lower west standards to 3rd world **depressed**,
will our water & **black** gold be sold in a global high bid contest?

Chorus:

War duels over fossil fuels, global **warmin'** & twisters stormin',
forests gone, no fish to spawn, earth to **desert** we're transformin'.
Oceans risin,' we're realisin' poor **clean** water can't afford o drink,
is it later than we think to **flush** pollution down a carbon sink?
Human multiplication **causin'** vulnerable species' decimation,
is god's ultimate creation & steward, **deserving** of damnation?

CAREERS – This Rant Goes Like Randy Travis' "Three Wooden Crosses."

My progeny, all **beaureaucrats** will be,
to survive **intact**, their grandchildren to see.

I will not **prostitute** them unto manual labour,
if it pays no more than their **office** neighbour.

The work is hard, weather uncertain, hazard **high**,
sick pay & **security**, in free enterprise don't apply.

A dillar a dollar, **maybe** a sometime scholar,
but **never** a forest industry west coast tree faller.

Chorus: Crippled, broken body, **racked** in pain,
        had I to live it over, I'd **never** do it again.

Should they **starve** to write a best seller shaker
or gamble at **contract** work & be a $ risk taker?

Perhaps an accredited, registered hospital nurse,
stressed, but not a **youthful** corpse in a hearse?

Choose careers to sustain you **before** you depart,
will even god **enable** you a living in music & art?

When **tenure** for English & math majors is rare,
opt for jobs in the **trades** where the pay is fair.

Chorus:
Don't invest years of study **incurring** a student loan
for vocations without a **union** umbrella safety zone.

Go where profit's **not** a must, no need to compete,
opt for secure air conditioned comfort on **easy** street.

Use the 18 days maximum sick pay allotted for it,
take **stress** time off & work overtime, fill your mitt.

Reap indexed pension & **bonus** if it earns more,
taxes replenish government's horn of plenty store.

Chorus:
If civil service retirees get **70**% pension at age 52,
is export industry that determines $ **value**, overdue**?**

If public sector were all Brit, Protestant & **white**,
would black majority protest that all is **not** right?

"What we have we **wish** for others," is labour motto,
but is the goal more **elusive** than winning the lotto?

Price of pioneering & misadventure are **final** & fast,
industrial casualties can **exceed** wars present & past.

Chorus:
When labour achieves the **One** Big Union dream,
of a field that's **level** with the civil service team,
where "Each earns according to his **ability** & need,"
so survivalists can feed & **super** achievers succeed.

When wages are **commensurate** with the task,
then my kin unto outdoor employment, I **may** ask,
for they **also** serve that sup off pork barrel plate,
dining on **taxpayer** flesh, never tempting fate.

Chorus:
When bureaucracy **fails** supply-demand of state,
when we can't **heat** homes & run to Mexico's gate,
will cushy paper shuffling & sweat **have** to relate
so those that can, **will** & the rest get a fair wage rate?

LOGGING CAMPS – ("Kisses Sweeter Than Wine" Tune.)

CHORUS: When I was a young man, I wanted to savour life,
before settling down to boredom of kids & a wife.

"Come west young fellers to big trees in logging camps,
they're looking for long term stakers, not saddle tramps."

Single girls from the cookhouse, too sought men,
dangling tempting breast fruits, time & again.

Chorus:
The manager gave orders that loggers he hired to log,
if any females came in heat, he was the top dog.

The push's daughter relished a bunkhouse bed,
to keep crews, supers saw they needed more than bread.

Chorus:
The daughter's beau really had something on the ball,
within a month his skill made him the best logger of all.

Seniority wasn't for promotion, only layoff & recall,
it was not what you knew but who, that made one tall.

Chorus:
I found a lock, fit the key & am grandfather of three,
marriage wasn't always ecstasy to nth degree,
but the self made alternative, never appealed to me.

MESSIAHS, pissing on peasants

Japan **lost** their yen for BC's high quality lumber in 1998,
with no other markets nor promised NDP bailout, the IWA **awaited** fate.

Amidst crashing world economies, expanding parks & **shrinking** forests gloom,
came a **saviour** CEO, crossed the US. border, to save us from impending doom.

This **Messiah** was shareholder heaven sent, workers were the **ransom** price,
to spark MB's revival, employees were **expendable** & tossed like dice.

BC's golden egg-laying goose, was **choking** on high stumpage & low yen,
NDP resolution for pensions from stumpage vanished in a **back** room den,
FRBC* splurged on education & administration, **woodworkers** lost again.

In the past, co-manage **incentive** plans by the IWA were considered sin,
now suddenly, this was deemed the very **best** partnership to be in.

For a small buy-out & a pension that could be cut, it was **cheap**,
with seniors pastured off & co-manage crews, labour's **lulled** to sleep.

In this uncertain climate of **shrinking** IWA labour pay check gloom,
a $500.00/month raise for **national** union executives was skunk perfume.

Although the sun is **setting** on sustained wood yield & forests forever,
officers organize non-wood sector, ensuring **their** pension won't sever.

Was IWA for years in **stagnation** studying locals' amalgamation,
did union officers join big union to avert **their** decimation?

If workers' rights can't be achieved, is justice **feigned** to be done,
did corporate haggard elite unity, result in **personal** gains won?

Did we once **abandon** an international, in a Union Jack dispute,
then to shed a **dictator,** the Munroe doctrine in steel we refute?

Did Mulroney's Eastern Canada free trade **benefits,** spell BC defeat,
did lobbyists pass raw log exports & **render** our sawmills obsolete?

If our **taxes** retire public sector after 30 years, on 70% indexed pension,
should **joining** civil service **O**ne **B**ig **U**nion, be private sector intention?

*FRBC – Forest Resources British Columbia

ON TOP OF THE OLD LOKEY

On top of the old lokey, all laden with **rust**,
are the **spirits** of old woodworkers, turned to dust.

From the east came young men to **join** the IWA,
they worked for many years to earn good pay,
but **today's** pension contributions with union may stay.
55 year old pension fathers didn't start the plan day **one**,
because pension they would merit hardly **none**,
so **we're** paying for all their years in the wood industry,
we have incurred **their** unfunded pension liability.

Even when vested this retirement plan had **no** heart,
if you didn't **survive** to 55, your family got no start.
This clause was **mercifully** later removed,
but as industry downsized, liability had **not** improved.

If you aren't **yet** collecting a pension,
you may need a **new** life extension,
because if the **unfunded** plan goes bust,
in **God,** young workers will have to trust.
Though pension contributions are a **deferred** wage,
the unvested **couldn't** from the plan their $ disengage.

Annual allowable cut hasn't proven **self**-sustaining,
is there even 10 years old growth **remaining**?
Where did all the stumpage dough go,
did administration bureaucracy, 20,000 BC forest jobs **blow**?
If stumpage & workers' taxes, **government** benefits guarantees,
why not put **stumpage** to pensions for labour on those trees?
On top of the old lokey, all **covered** with rust,
are the spirits of old **woodworkers**, now dust.

Gone are the days of Auld Lang Syne,
retirement gold watch & all that's **holy** & divine.
Forgotten is export industry that **earns** foreign currency,
is the fabled level playing field **swamped** in bureaucracy?
Tamed & obsolete now is labour's weapon, the wildcat,
no more mortal combat, mediation is where it's at.
Numbers determine who gets biggest cut of country's **economic** pie,
for government unions, indexed pensions & bonus they **justify**
but private enterprise worker will get **his,** in the bye and bye.

When a policeman is killed, it **raises** the country's ire,
when woodworkers **fall**, only the locals inquire.
Industrial **casualty** stats are akin to war,
wet & sweat in every pore but **few** benefits we score.
Risking life & limb, in flies, deluge & cold each day,
if you don't **survive**, you won't collect your pay.
Loggers & mill workers are **common**, cannon fodder,
when supply outweighs demand, we're **cheap** to slaughter.
This endangered species, will just **have** to get by,
squeegeeing, diving for **tourist** pennies or to Alberta fly,
before meeting their **final** arbiter in the sky.

Play jeopardy, be a **risk** taker,
reap **posthumous** prize from your maker
but if your job should give you **stress**,
no early retirement, do **you** possess.
Executives may reap the **lion's** share of the spoil
but even public service pays **more** than contract toil.
On top of the **old** lokey, all laden with rust,
are **spirits** of old woodworkers, turned to dust.

Come hither young maidens, **heed a** parent's plea,
marry a woodworker and the breadwinner **you** may be.
For even with changes & a pension that's **not** in red,
a **sunset** industry future, we all dread.

While MLA & MP puppets are **passing** the buck,
BC endangered wood industry is getting a **royal**….
Is a low stumpage BC tree, free trade's **sacrificial** goat,
to **placate** the East majority & ensure their vote?
Log exports render pulp & sawmills as fish cannery row,
if socialists ran the show, could **they** call a whoa?

Like locusts, US corporations **denude** our Eden,
log sales **don't** create the jobs/cubic meter of Sweden.
Have we squandered our heritage & dealt industry a **death** blow ,
must woodworkers join miners, fishermen & the extinct **dodo**?
On top of the old lokey, all **covered** with rust,
ride the spirits of old woodworkers, turning over in **disgust.**

It's a strange, **strange** world we live in, master Jack,
for hazard & bushel work, woodsmen are coloured **black,**
parity with pulp mills & government they lack.
Should export workers that **earn** our country's wealth,
be denied government benefits & depend on their **health**?

On 2nd growth, our industry was made **lean** & bled,
as national union officers on a $500. monthly raise, **regally** fed.
A false-hearted lover may be **worse** than a thief,
but blind faith in haggard **Judases**, causes grief.

Are Liberals traitors , forest-mill ties to sever & undo,
should **auctioning** tree farm land for high bid, be taboo?
Is it an election debt that **must** be repaid & is overdue
to profit the few more from logs than lumber, will they rue?

Railroad, steamboat, river & **canal**,
yonder comes a steel man, has he **conned** our IWA* pal?
Is it an international favouring USA with feet of **clay**,
is it a straw union too **weak** to arrest forest decay?
Is it another elaborate retirement **scheme**,
funding **elites'** pensions, skimming off old growth cream
or symbiosis, fulfilling a One Big **Red** Union dream?

Will we gain if we join **public** sector's mainstream
reap their gold standard of an **indexed** pension supreme?
If IWA had public sector 18 day annual sick pay,
would sickness take up the time allotted to it without delay?

Since the Red **socialist** empire has died,
youth in **great** numbers on today's streets reside.
With world **free** trade, will welfare always provide,
can middle class **survive**, its downhill slide,
with no trees to hew, will drawing water instil pride?

Pensioned seniors "Have **gone** away on a jet plane"
but will our children's heritage be **good** times again?
The **pioneers** of oceans, mines, valley, woodland & hill,
lie moulding **unacknowledged** & the forest is still.
We never logged but **mined**, in insane profit lust,
did we **betray** old union organizers' trust?
On top of the old lokey, all covered with rust,
Spirits of woodworkers moan, is change for the worse a must?

Forests forever & sustained yield are faint slogans of the past,
we knew high grading old growth could never last.
Loggers' cook & bunkhouses are gone & they're no longer bussed,
each corporate trader profited & the industry is bust.
Employees are no longer considered a company resource,
contractors save 10% holiday pay, getting rid of the old work horse,
shuffled like cards, no one has seniority in the now work force.
Animal rights ensure that work elephants are retired at 45
but man is a work mule, hitched to the plough to 65.

If overpopulated resource poor Europe's standard of living
is higher than ours, are our politicians to corporations more giving?
On top of the old lokey, all covered with **rust**,
the spirits of woodworkers wail, "Is **this** just?"

*IWA – **I**nternational **W**oodwsorkers of **A**merica

The attempted medley of several tunes is an example of what some industrial pension plans were like, before there was sufficient funding for improvement. Unlike most government plans, there's no minimum guarantee in the event of another stock market crash nor indexing & bonus.

POOR BASHIN' – tune?

While **honest** men labour & high taxes must pay,
the underground economy **secretes** theirs away.

Workers sweat & **shiver** in hovels to save every cent,
if low rental units aren't metered, **our** taxes they vent.

While workers, **life** term mortgages must endure,
 should habitat homes low **interest** be only for the poor?
if they sell their habitat & **blow** the dough,
back on the welfare plan, are they **free** to go?

Dog food, **vet**s, lawyers & cigarettes workers procure,
but for the leisure class, does **social** assistance assure?

Your labour **may** provide a family dental plan,
can **others** get it free from the government man?

When cities tax home **improvement**, slums arise,
yet **service** costs are the same for lots of equal size.

Gamblers, addicts & artists **don't** work, we lament,
yet get counsel & grants & OAP **supplements** rent.

Workers drug tests endure but injection is addict cure,
we import farm labour, yet able bodied, dole procure.

If with RRSP & private pensions, **you** can retire,
your Canada pension, the taxman may acquire,
& retirement homes, **more** from the haves require.

If govt's umbrella is a **prophylactic** rain preventive,
from cradle to grave, should 'spend' be our incentive?

Did our culture's grasshopper that **fiddled** & played,
prove wiser than the ant that **slaved** & taxes paid?

TARGET – sung to "Angel Band."

CHORUS: My industry's sun is **sinking** fast, my race is nearly run,
since my journey first begun, tougher trials are **yet** to come.

Falling, mining & fishing was lucrative **contract** work,
sweat & hazard on a good day got **more** than a city clerk.

With today's **free** trade, raw material goes for highest bid,
must West's labour **cut rate**, or face a 3rd world skid?

Can we hope to salvage organized labour's **middle** class,
or revert to past history's opulent class & **poor** mass?

Chorus:

Do senior workers have **targets** painted on their back,
do corporations regard 15% holiday pay as seniority plaque?

Is it like another Canada's **Asian** discrimination act repeat,
even if productivity's high, do employers **dump** labour elite?

"**Survival** of the fittest" in capitalism & nature is steeled,
would benefits parity for young & old, **level** the playing field?

Chorus:

Should only **public** service get indexed pension guarantee,
will security for private enterprise be **denied** for eternity?

"What we desire for ourselves, we **wish** for all" is union motto,
will **parity** with government workers be sure as winning lotto?

Must workers **homeless** upon the streets be forced to roam,
& await angel band to carry us away to our **immortal** home?

Chorus:

TO A CORPORATE LOUSE

CHORUS: Eh grinning, **greedy,** overstuffed beastie,
    'tis off **workers'** blood that ye feastie.

Toil ye **not**, nor sweat nor sow,
yet untold rewards to **thee** doth flow.
Tho a worker's lot be a thousandth of thy **worth**,
'twas earned by sweat & strife, **not** thru birth.

Labour's **hazards** ye doth not know,
thine kin, their true mettle **kenna** show,
spooned in silver, they donna see,
workers' **stubborn** pride, so unlike thee.

Chorus:
Capitalism **spurned** Communism altruism
for **greed** be a greater motivator than socialism.
If to **question** capitalist stability be heresy,
is prophecy of depression **proven** history?

When CEOs **fail**, state rushes in socialist aid,
corporate welfare be our **trickle** down bandaid?
Was state owned means of production so wrong,
 with no homeless nor rich, resources to all belong

Your news media manufacture political consent
& stringed **puppet** politicians collect the rent.
Free trade $ **chase,** all middle class gains erase,
we **fall** from grace, finish last in 3rd world race?

Chorus:
When kin only love or **murder** for thine worth,
is it better to have little but **peace** on earth?
Oh Lord the gift, that he would but **give** us,
to see the future & **bypass** the path so grievous.

'tis not upon **this** world, labour be dealt squarely,
but comes a reckoning when **all** be judged fairly.
Nepotism's Good Ole Boy corrupt corporate turf,
in the grave's hereafter may be of **little** worth.
Chorus:

TO A LABOUR LOUSE

Ha, ya big bad **brawlin'** beastie,
'tis off the **corporate** class ye feastie.

Ya **bemoan** the servitude of a wage slave,
but forget that no **poor** man, ever a job gave.

From the cradle to thy **commoner** grave
secure in union contract, for **naught** ye crave.

Working 9 to 5 with **no** management strife,
stress-**free**, ye trod on home to your wife.

Though your living standards be the **best**,
in thy company, nary a cent do **you** invest.

If not for bank & **corporate** ties with politicians,
there would be 1929 stock **crash** repetitions.

The pendulum of time, too far **left** has swung,
without correction, we're 3rd World **dung**.

Government union monopoly extort **too** high a fee,
with no need to compete, no **onus** for profitability,
taxpayers' **flesh** is shred & bled near bankruptcy.

Capitalists **spurned** the altruism of Communism
because **greed** is a greater motivator than socialism.

The fittest **thrive** in nature, sports & export industry,
job security must not on seniority but **performance** be,
lest we get soft & ne'er evolve to the **best** we can be.

Since we both be bound in a union-corporate **seal**,
in symbiotic sustainability, we must **honour** our deal.

If **money** & connections here, have served us well,
Lord the gift he give - a **Good** Ole Boy Club in hell!

WHICH SIDE ARE YOU ON – Labour tune

My momma was a **health** care worker,
my daddy laboured in the **mill**.
Today both are **outa** work,
job & **log** exports make BC ill.

The **fat** cats & average Joes
got a liberal, **percentage** tax break,
but medicare, hydro & education **hikes**,
took the icing off workers' **hobo** cake.

CHORUS: The rich-poor gap's **awidenin**,
                  the downtrodden **hafta** organize.
                  Labour & poor are but **one** caste,
                  we'd all be wise to **fraternize**.

Last election, **workers** caste their vote,
that day, we now **surely** rue,
wages are gettin' levelled **down**,
3rd world child labour gets BC **debut**.

Don't **scab** for free enterprise,
don't be **suckered** by their lies.
Don't **kiss** any capitalist ass,
don't **whore** for the corporate class.

Chorus:

Now all you **indebted** students,
mortgagin' futures to stay in school,
tuition increases don't **hurt** the wealthy,
so don't you be their protégé nor **tool**.

Politicians piss on peasants, media **call** it rain,
when **all** are homeless, is it levelling the plane?
Is free trade **final** solution ruling elite proclaim,
when they **come** for us, who's left to cry "Shame"?

Chorus:

WORKERS' LAMENT

How grand it is for the **leisure** class to get low rental,
worker's taxes pay their medical & sometimes **even** dental.

But if school uniforms, lunches & housing are the **same**,
then is labour's drudgery & dole's **free** ride an uneven game?

While household pets & unemployed **watch** their favourite TV show,
in deluge, heat, flies, wind, rain or snow, wage slaves **daily** go,
if uninjured, return to mow the lawn, sleep & **start** another day again,
the holiday caste **relax** in safety, shouldn't reward merit strain?

Communists **manifest** "Each according to his ability & need,"
do we sustain survivalists but **tax** super achievers that succeed?

Chance befall **all** but to whom much is given, much is expected
can't the **least** of society's able for farm labour be selected?

How we make our bed, so we lie, or must some for others atone,
do the poor & rich dine off our flesh, be they **parasite** or drone?

If to hold a job, workers must **pass** industry sobriety drug test
& chiefs evict reserves' addicts, can **injection** sites be blessed?

If nations overpopulate beyond their land's **ability** to provide,
can we feed them **worldwide** or will we again witness genocide?

If government's **Big Union** indexed pensions **lead** the way,
should private sector unions **merge** with them without delay?

If ant & grasshopper must end in the **same** care home in old age,
should those that slaved & saved, **surrender** their sweat wage?

If the world's riches were divided & to all **equally** doled out,
within a year would the **same** have-nots be again without?

Can 21st century West all our **social** advances maintain,
will free trade starve **welfare**, can the middle class remain?

AUTHOR

How did they market a lie of **biblical** proportion,
were weapons of **mass** destruction the extortion?

Is safeguarding energy supplies the **ultimate** prize,
are complex **pretexts** & lies we forced to devise?

Are we **mesmerized** by orators, religion or greed,
can we be lead to commit any **despicable** deed?

Demagogues promote unproven policy to **please** majority,
are clergy sorority **given** the authority to make it priority?

Do we believe that to **presidents**, god does talk,
are lemmings steered **off** the path of the peace walk?

Would psychiatrists agree war is **creator's** command,
do we pretend to **defend** our country on foreign land?

Just as the chosen, **killed** Canaanites for promised land,
must America **bloody** their hand to secure oil sand?

When US monkey trial **permitted** teaching of evolution,
why are atheist politicians **closeted** to avoid persecution?

Can we by **our** own hand, Armageddon's rapture realize
logic defies, does the herd instinct lead to our demise?

THE CANUCK TOTEM POLE

At the very top are the Aboriginals, the Brahman or highest caste,
after treaties will schooling, housing, hunting & fishing rights last?

Next are the Metis & Quebecois of a special status & unique,
with education assistance & language rights - another privileged clique?
Then public service indexed pensions & welfare's paid legal fees,
is paying for their perks, Canada' national social disease?

At the foot of the totem, are the untouchables, the common Canucks,
so politically naive, we support this hierarchy with our tax bucks.
Did Quebec Referendum fail because the Canadian majority,
refused to perpetuate this system of the privileged minority?

Natives are stuck on reserves but inherit aboriginal rights & land,
would a treaty signing bonus provide an incentive to disband?
If we pay the natives, Metis & Quebecois **all** their rights to surrender,
will this unify us under one language & be a multiculture blender?

If partial caste removal per BC resident is only $1.60, make it $1.61
to emancipate all common Canucks & see the people's will be done.
Can we save on self-government's doubling bureaucracy cost,
to increase medicare, welfare & prevent lives from being lost?

Shades of Bouchard & Riel, our bloody past have we forgot,
to safeguard culture, must history repeat & civil war be fought?
Does assimilation give us a common language of communication,
can we bypass religious & racial persecution, through integration?

Will we meld our feudal lords into a great Canuck melting pot,
lest the world's lessons on ethnic holocausts, be all for naught?
To grant all equal seating on our Canuck bus, would require a magician,
renail Jim Crow's coffin & reincarnate a Rosa Parks reform politician.

GRAY POWER

Born post WWII, jobs are plentiful & boomers earn **top** union rates,
with no lean years, we've got RSP's, pension & sup on **silver** plates.

With transportation, restaurant, property tax & insurance **discounts**,
staying home, babysitting grandchildren, the bank balance **mounts**.

Canada Pension we may drain but gray power lobbies for **more**,
living longer, do we **take** what our kin put in & deplete their store?

Penniless in youth, we only **dreamed** of candy, travel & booze,
age diminishes the taste of what's now affordable, so we just **snooze**.

Society functions in **reverse**, by the time the house is paid, we're in decay,
workers that save until they're old & gray, in retirement homes **must** pay.

Hunter gatherers were **forced** to abandon sedentary elders to starvation,
is red circling seniors youth's **minimum** wage sentence & exploitation?

Have unions desecrated nature's survival of the **fittest** that served eternity,
in monopolizing work, have we created a **Good Ole Boy** Fraternity?

Should seniority be the **sole** criteria for 50 years of career security,
aren't natural resources to be **shared**, so none die jobless in obscurity?

Is seniors' death grip on jobs to buy motorhomes & boats, **age** discrimination,
we fought no wars, built no unions, are we history's **chosen**, favoured generation?

Economist Galbraith counseled "Comfort the afflicted & **afflict** the comfortable,"
should we **level** field, our progeny enable & tax the seniors that had it so stable?

Workers raising kids, keep the economy **humming** & money's in circulation,
is leaving youth 20 years work to **raise** our grandchildren, fair compensation?

HUMILITY - "Oh Lord it's hard to be humble."

Was it the '**Good** Ole Boy Club' or a casting couch for the arts,
that gave mortals their starts in a **stellar** rise topping the charts?
Are the top sellers always the vintage of the **best** told tales,
are beer palates **fit** to judge if champagne passes or fails?

Chorus: Lord, it's hard to **humble** authors so **perfect** in every way,
               does talent elevate them to literary **godhood** & photo display?

Are the arts **pearls** before swine, on commoners a waste,
are critics deemed connoisseurs to **mould** culture & taste?
Without them, would we by "Mona Lisa" be **impressed**,
are fans nude emperors out to ace an **intelligence** test?

Chorus:
Can all judges like disc jockeys be tempted by **bribes** or gifts,
to makeover **near**-do-wells through media's hypnotic facelifts?
Are sales agents bible punchers flogging works inspired by **gods**,
does public buy books to **prove** they're not ignorant clods?

Chorus:
Psychiatrists say we **all** vent poetry at some point or event
but can it be considered talent if it can't even pay the rent?
Could the words or the skill be mystical & truly **profound**,
are they testament prophecy, **meant** to astound & confound?

Chorus:
Could artists & clergy survive **capitalist** supply & demand,
would they exist without government's subsidizing **hand**?
When the lobster whistles or when god **pays** musicians,
means it will **never** happen, so say European politicians.

How many hippy flowers blush unseen on desert sands,
is talent wasted without $20 fee that CBC* contest demands?
We **revere** academia & worship monuments to the past,
writers can **lie** for a living but labour's reality is downcast.
If food, shelter & health are priorities, faith & **culture** last,
is there no **recognition** for work that's sweaty & low caste?

*CBC is radio Canadian Broadcasting Corporation.

INVADERS

Invaders bloodied green, arable, inhabited shores,
raiding, raping, **plundering** their resource stores.

A century later, even more **ruthless** conquerors came,
& vanquished those that to the **first** nations did the same.

Every aggressor seeded the pool & was **steeled** in war,
underdogs before, they swore "Britons be slaves **no** more."

Pillage & theft are not acts **exclusive** only to white,
in nature, territory is disputed, it's a **rite** of might,
victor takes all, in retreat one **forfeits** all right.

Overpopulation **spurs** exploration & natural selection
culls those **not** immune to any new viral infection.

Unified in language & faith, the world they **sought** to get,
carved continents for an empire on which the sun **never** set

History's witnessed **other** lands' holocausts, suffering & pain,
Canadian justice shoots **word** bullets, tax $ are victims slain,
lawyers will arbitrate as long as negotiations **we** sustain.

LEGAL COUNSEL

Shyster, shabbits, solicitor, trustworthy as a car dealer or politician,
freeing murderers & rapists, as ethical as a salesman on commission.

For years they train in the costly legal arts of tongue-fu,
contracts coded in legalese lingo, foreign to average me & you.

    Conjuring up injuries that doctors say don't even exist,
    to win high commissions, bucking probability they persist.

    If the guilty client's trials are delayed & bail they can provide,
    it's through the skill of their mouthpiece that justice is denied.

        Probate fees are more lucrative on percentage than a per hour basis,
        & divorce cost is not just an hourly fee but bonus for winning cases.

        If attorneys appear greedy & ruthless throwback from primeval,
        are they supply & demand's piranhas & society's **necessary** evil?

Clients procure justice according to the wealth of the family coffer,
democracy's inequitable but for the poor is it the best it can offer?

Sanitary engineers remove garbage & clean up the city's streets,
does judicial system recycle & filter humanity's wastes & cheats?

        Defending molesters & debauchers, is the most distasteful of chores,
        would killing all the lawyers, necessitate a return to duels, strikes & wars?

        If to legal beagles with words for ammunition, generals had to report,
        could warfare be waged on the battlefields of United Nations world court?

MARIJUANA MARTYR, Requiem for Mark Emery.

Is marijuana like martini, a bad habit we can't reverse,
have nicotine & alcohol proved addicting & even worse?

Pot & peyote ceremonial use are legal in religious service
but without prescription, possession makes us nervous.

Even for casual use of THC, there's no defense or plea
& for USA repeat offenders, they throw away the key.

If US toquers double Holland's lawful consumption,
is **forbidden** fruit filling demand, a logical assumption?

Uncle Sam's troops puffed the weed while in Viet Nam,
Moslems hasheshed in Afghanistan & no one gave a dam.

There's no extradition in Britain for cannabis seed sales,
are threats of border closures just US scare tactic tales?

Laws are enforced only with compliance of majority
& a joint seed sale levy was **collected** by tax authority.

Al Capone **evaded** taxes, can Mark Emery be his peer,
do we end his career or offer sanctuary to our pot pioneer?

Countries allow gambling, run lotteries & bootleg booze,
if these are Christian values, what more have we to lose?

Is legalization the goal & our marijuana martyr the toll,
will Prince of Pot cut a deal to save his immortal soul?

If to harass grass is to cover ass, is it a self interest view,
if bud was not taboo, could we downsize the justice crew?

Is it an archaic religious law like no playing ball on Sunday
that California may legislate & make all users tax pay?

To erace the deficit & replenish our depleted treasury,
should BC get wise & legalize our 2nd biggest industry?

Will Campbell choke democracy & dictator for his term be,
let referendum decide - a tax on hemp decree or pay HST?

HST is Harmonized Sales Tax enacted on meals & services in BC.

PROSPECTIVE POLITICIAN – not for the faint of heart.

As honest as a lawyer & as trustworthy as a car salesman,
on **straight** unbiased answers, have politicians declared a ban,
is truth an unaffordable luxury that could **offend** their bag man?
Parties select the best candidates, they **have** to be squeaky clean,
they want **stars** on ice to score points for their political machine.
your **life** is a pubic book & the least indiscretion is judged obscene.

Left or right, one slip of lip & you're a pariah, a **social** disease,
yet switching capitalist ties for assured election, **isn't** sleaze,
you're a pro athlete, a gladiator with expertise & a **new** team please.
Is the contract only **traitorous** when flipping from right to socialist
that you've betrayed your class & are labelled a rank **opportunist**,
does going the other way **open** ambition's doors, that didn't exist?

Never **apologize** for being wealthy, even if through ill-gotten gain,
for the country believes electing a poor man, borders on the **insane**.
Voters trusted Kennedy & Trudeau, for **their** country they cut a deal,
unlike Lian Bull-roney, to live high, they didn't **have** to steal.
With no seniority, cast bread upon troubled waters & **placate** majority,
insert foot in mouth & even leaders lose favour in **their** sorority.
To survive two terms, you must get the rabble's **undivided** attention,
patronize, commit to **nothing**, it's the safest route to a life pension.

If atheists be without authority, mention **god** in speech like your peers,
snow dark ages' moral majority to allay party burned at stake fears.
Presidents **don't** wield dictatorship absolute power in our democracy,
to **please** aristocracy, they alienate minority, it's bureaucracy hypocrisy.
Kim Campbell's* double digit unemployment **pained** electorate ears,
bearers of bad news are no longer **shot**, public just ends their careers.

Treating all provinces justly & **fairly** is not a foreseeable probability,
if Ontario & Quebec's majority isn't placated, governing is **impossibility**.
For votes, fractionalise the country, grant favours to **secessionist** rebels,
for party funding, sell your soul & barter with those **lobbyist** devils.

To accomplish great deeds, may mean **lying** thru your teeth to get selected,
had Abe Lincoln ran as an **abolitionist**, would he have been elected,
did Tommy Douglas pass **medicare** & see his party for years rejected?
Shakespeare said "Oh devious webs we weave, as we **practice** to deceive,"
is "The end **justifies** the means," a maxim priests & politicians perceive?

*Kim Campbell –interim successor to Prime Minister Mulroney that caused Conservatives' defeat.

SQUATTERS

If workers must buy or rent only where they can afford,
are choice low rent areas & food banks failure's reward?
If supply & demand no longer suits society's need,
then why not grant every citizen a property deed?

If we continue to enable all present drug addicted,
what's the incentive to quit & can others be afflicted?
Could leper colony isolation be addict medication,
would this be salvation for the majority population?

Migrants from towns, to big cities annually come,
without jobs to pay rent, to streets they succumb.
Bed & breakfasting on sidewalks is **not** a right,
beggars on tourist posters aren't an appealing sight.

If the world's wealth to all was equally doled out,
in a year would the have-nots be again without?
Some can never store disposable income away
& depend on government's umbrella each rainy day.
If the poor must always be with us, as Christ said,
could the able do farm labour & earn their daily bread?

To whom much was given, much may be expected,
will those that took more than they put in, be rejected,
is it by grace or works that for paradise we're selected?

THERE'S A **BLACK** MAN IN THE **WHITE** HOUSE !
Tune – This Old House.

Guard the stores, too late to shutter the windows & **bar** the doors,
a **black** man's in the white house, who'll do the manual chores?

This old house withstood Democrat & Republican procession,
the roof's been subjected to on, off & back on solar obsession.

The house weathered secession, depression & forced confession,
trembled in Mcarthyism, Alzheimer & moral majority oppression.

Chorus:
Gotta make this house stronger, our kin will be here eons longer,
how will we ever explain if those Canucks burn it down again?

For years it saw no colour & locked atheist politician out,
can a devout president of African racial descent, have clout?

Will the South secede & the white knights burn crosses again,
will old wounds fester or progeny see a colour blind campaign?

Will those rednecks approve a medical plan from a black man,
or back insurance lobbies & ring in McArthy era socialist ban?

Chorus:
Gotta make this house stronger, our kin will be here eons longer,
how will we ever explain if those Canucks burn it down again?

Since time began, the white man curled hair & got a sun tan,
geneticists confirmed **who** put the curl in noble Roman clan.

Professional sports broke the code, ended colour discrimination,
they chose the best & left the rest to sue for % representation.

This old house is tattered & worn, heaped with **justified** scorn,
torn to **draft** god in oil war, has a new day dawned, is it reborn?

Chorus:
Gotta make this house stronger, our kin will be here eons longer,
how will we ever explain if those Canucks burn it down again?

FUNERAL for a LOUSE

The gold inlaid, embossed coffin was covered in spit,
his peers paid only the respects that society would permit.

Not even all of his closest blood kin were there,
nor heir did despair, they were there to claim their share.

The priest didn't abandon a family in their time of need,
an elderly loving mother & a blindly loyal wife he did heed.

The corporation & nation made it a media sensation,
their collaboration ensured there was no public revelation.

The country will mourn another son worthy of castration,
voters paid for corporate cuts during his administration.

Biblically, only the poor were stoned for adultery,
for a fee to RC, rich could be ransomed from purgatory.

It should be no surprise, it's as American as apple pie
that for a price, respectability even you & I can buy.

One can bury the truth & get amnesty for a donation,
rich don't divorce but get annulment by papal dispensation.

Can death alone, atone for such a high magnitude of sin
will hell-fire or reincarnation's karma, absolution win?